# THE OFFICIAL
# ASTON VILLA
## ANNUAL 2018

*Happy Birthday*
*Jimmy*
*2018*
*lots of love*
*Daddy !*

*UP THE VILLA !!*

**AVFC**

**Compiled by Rob Bishop**
**Designed by Uta Dohlenburg**

A Grange Publication

©2017. Published by Grange Communications Ltd., Edinburgh, under licence from Aston Villa Football Club. Printed in the EU.

Special thanks to Gayner Monkton.

Photographs © Neville Williams, Getty Images and PA Images.

ISBN: 978-1-911287-65-0

# CONTENTS

# CLUB HONOURS

## EUROPEAN CUP

**WINNERS:** 1981-82
**QUARTER-FINALISTS:** 1982-83

## EUROPEAN SUPER CUP

**WINNERS:** 1982-83

## WORLD CLUB CHAMPIONSHIP

**RUNNERS-UP:** 1982

## INTERTOTO CUP

**WINNERS:** 2001

## FOOTBALL LEAGUE

**CHAMPIONS:**
1893-94, 1895-96, 1896-97, 1898-99,
1899-1900, 1909-10, 1980-81

**RUNNERS-UP:**
1888-89, 1902-03, 1907-08, 1910-11,
1912-13, 1913-14, 1930-31, 1932-33,
1989-90

## PREMIER LEAGUE

**RUNNERS-UP:** 1992-93

## DIVISION TWO

**CHAMPIONS:** 1937-38, 1959-60

## DIVISION THREE

**CHAMPIONS:** 1971-72

## FA CUP

**WINNERS:**
1887, 1895, 1897, 1905, 1913, 1920, 1957

**RUNNERS-UP:**
1892, 1924, 2000, 2015

## LEAGUE CUP

**WINNERS:** 1961, 1975, 1977, 1994, 1996

**RUNNERS-UP:** 1963, 1971, 2010

## FA YOUTH CUP

**WINNERS:** 1972, 1980, 2002

**RUNNERS-UP:** 2004, 2010

## NEXTGEN SERIES

**WINNERS:** 2013

# THE NEW BOYS

## PLAY IT AGAIN, SAM!

remained at Villa Park for the second half of the 2016-17 season.

When the campaign ended, his future was unclear, but he was delighted to be offered the opportunity in July of a full season as a Villan.

"There was a lot of talk during the summer about where I might go," he said. "But I'm glad to be back. "I really enjoyed my time here last season and it was an easy decision to come back.

Sam Johnstone clearly doesn't believe in doing things by halves. He jumped at the chance of signing on the dotted line for Villa for the second time in seven months.

The 24-year-old keeper initially arrived on loan from Manchester United in January and

"To play at Villa Park in front of 30,000 or more is a great feeling. It was difficult when I came here in January but I settled in well.

"Coming back on loan for a full season, rather than half way through, will hopefully be a big help – and I'm delighted to be No 1!"

## ELMO'S 'HAT-TRICK'

He doesn't have a reputation as a prolific scorer but Ahmed Elmohamady netted a hat-trick when he joined Villa. It was the third time he has been signed by Steve Bruce! The manager and player also worked together at both Sunderland and Hull City, so Bruce didn't need to do much homework before making "Elmo" a Villa player.

"It's very exciting to come here because this is one of the biggest clubs in England," said the Egyptian winger. "I know Villa are in the Championship but I also know all about the history of the club.

"I've been with the gaffer for a long time. He brought me from Egypt to Sunderland and then to Hull and he's one of the best managers I've worked with.

"It's a great challenge to get back in the Premier League but I'm happy to be working with Steve again.

"He was a great player and he played for one of the biggest clubs in the world (Manchester United) so he knows what is needed."

## A NEW ADVENTURE...

Villa have boasted an impressive list of Republic of Ireland internationals down the years, Paul McGrath, Steve Staunton, Andy Townsend and Ray Houghton having made important contributions to the club's history.

And Glenn Whelan is hoping to follow in the footsteps of those claret-and-blue greats after signing a two-year contract with the club.

"A lot of Irish players have done well here," he said. "If I can do half as well as those lads it would be great."

The 33-year-old midfielder joined Villa after nine years with Stoke City, where he was hugely popular with supporters.

"I was at Stoke for a long time and enjoyed some happy times there," he said. "But I decided it was

time for a new adventure. I've played against most of the lads in the squad, and there's a lot of competition for places.

"We have players here who have played in the Premier League – and that's where we want to be."

## NICE TO SEE YOU – AGAIN!

New players sometimes take a while to get to know their team-mates but there was no such problem for Chris Samba. When he signed on the dotted line in July, the towering central defender had already been training with Villa since the start of the year.

Manager Steve Bruce agreed to Samba training at Bodymoor Heath after the former Blackburn and QPR player was released by Greek club Panathanaikos in January.

Samba impressed the boss with his work ethic, and was invited to join the squad at their pre-season training camp in Portugal. Then, after playing in a couple of pre-season friendlies he was handed a one-year contract. And almost as a thank-you, he scored against Hertha Berlin in the final of the Cup of Traditions in Germany three days later.

"I've played many times against Aston Villa," he said. "It's a club I have the greatest respect for because of its standing in the game."

## JOSH IS IN SAFE HANDS...

It speaks volumes for the quality of Villa's coaching staff that Josh Onomah was allowed to join the club on a season-long loan from Tottenham Hotspur.

The 20-year-old midfielder is highly rated at White Hart Lane and has signed a four-year contract with the London club.

Spurs manager Mauricio Pochettino is usually reluctant to let his promising youngsters go out on loan, preferring them to be nurtured by his own coaches. But he was happy to make an exception when Villa boss Steve Bruce enquired about Onomah – much to the player's delight.

"I'm very excited," said Onomah, who helped England to glory at the under-20 World Cup in South Korea during the summer. "I have high hopes of playing a lot of games, which is important for any young player.

"I enjoy dribbling, running with the ball, passing and shooting – and I'm looking to improve on all those things while I'm here. The gaffer told me he wants me to enjoy myself and play with freedom."

## ROBERT'S POSITIONAL SENSE

Robert Snodgrass became the second player to join Villa on loan from a London club when he signed from West Ham until the end of the season.

When it became apparent that the Scotland international was unlikely to feature in the Hammers' line-up, he was only too happy for a fresh start under the management of Steve Bruce, who was also his boss at Hull City.

"This was the only option for me because of the manager and the backroom team, who I have worked with before," he said.

"I was played out of position at West Ham but the manager knows where I am at my best. I like to play wide on the right or just behind the striker. I will try to be the best person I can, both on the park and on the training ground.

"Loyalty is a big thing. Steve was a big help to me when I was injured at Hull. He got me back to where I wanted to be."

# SIGNING OF THE SUMMER!

People often say that the best things in life are free – and Villa certainly hope that will prove to be the case with the club's first summer signing of 2017.

Former England captain John Terry had reached the end of his contract with Premier League champions Chelsea, so he was available on a free transfer.

And despite interest from a number of other clubs, he chose to sign for Villa on a one-year contract.

That prompted a host of favourable comments from former Villans, including Dean Saunders, the striker who topped our goal charts for three consecutive seasons in the early 1990s.

Saunders posted a message on Twitter, comparing Terry's arrival at Villa Park with striker Romelu Lukaku's reported £75m move from Everton to Manchester United.

"Forget Lukaku going to Man United," said Deano, "John Terry to Villa is the signing of the summer."

But it's not only strikers who appreciate Terry's experience and solid defensive qualities. Ex-Villa defender Carlos Cuellar was equally impressed with the transfer.

"What a legend!" tweeted the Spaniard. "John Terry arrives at my @AVFCOfficial. I wish you all the best and I'm sure you will enjoy the experience of being a Villan."

Terry won a host of top honours at Stamford Bridge, helping Chelsea to five triumphs in both the Premier League and the FA Cup, as well as the League Cup (three times), the Champions League and the Europa League.

Now we're all hoping he can play a big part in leading Villa back into English football's top flight.

Albert Adomah

# MY VERY FIRST...

*There's a first time for everything, and footballers are no exception. Villa's players tell us about their "firsts".*

## JAMES CHESTER

| | |
|---|---|
| **Team:** | WINICK ATHLETIC |
| **Replica shirt:** | Probably MANCHESTER UNITED |
| **Game watched:** | MAN UNITED v ROTOR VOLGOGRAD, 1995 |
| **Car:** | VAUXHALL CORSA |
| **Pet:** | A BLACK LABRADOR, BESSIE |

## CONOR HOURIHANE

| | |
|---|---|
| **Team:** | BANDON AFC |
| **Replica shirt:** | BRAZIL |
| **Game watched:** | THE 1998 WORLD CUP |
| **Album:** | LIMP BIZKIT – ROLLIN' |
| **Pet:** | A CAT CALLED WHISKERS |

## MILE JEDINAK

| | |
|---|---|
| **Team:** | WERRINGTON CROATIA (AUSTRALIA) |
| **Replica shirt:** | AC MILAN |
| **Game watched:** | AUSTRALIA v MILAN, 1990 |
| **Car:** | HOLDEN COMMODORE VT |
| **Pet:** | A ROTTWEILER CALLED ROXY |

## HENRI LANSBURY

| | |
|---|---|
| **Team:** | POTTERS BAR UNITED |
| **Replica shirt:** | INTER MILAN |
| **Game watched:** | ENGLAND v CHILE |
| **Football hero:** | FAUSTINO ASPRILLA |
| **Pet:** | A RABBIT CALLED GILBERT |

## SCOTT HOGAN

| | |
|---|---|
| **Team:** | CADISHEAD SPORTS |
| **Replica shirt:** | MAN UNITED |
| **Game watched:** | MAN UNITED v COVENTRY 1996 |
| **Football hero:** | ERIC CANTONA |
| **Pet:** | A DOG CALLED MILTON |

## JAMES BREE

| | |
|---|---|
| **Team:** | WAKEFIELD UNITED |
| **Replica shirt:** | It was either LIVERPOOL or LEEDS UNITED! |
| **Game watched:** | LIVERPOOL v NEWCASTLE, 2006 |
| **Car:** | VW SCIROCCO |
| **Pet:** | A GOLDFISH |

## JACK GREALISH

| | |
|---|---|
| **Team:** | HIGHGATE UNITED |
| **Replica shirt:** | VILLA – WHEN I WAS THREE! |
| **Football hero:** | CRISTIANO RONALDO |
| **Game watched:** | VILLA 3 LEEDS 2 IN THE FA CUP, 2000 |
| **Pet:** | A CAT CALLED TIMOTHY |

## ANDRE GREEN

| | |
|---|---|
| **Team:** | SOILHULL JUNIORS |
| **Replica shirt:** | MANCHESTER UNITED |
| **Game watched:** | A WREXHAM GAME! |
| **Car:** | MERCEDES A-CLASS |
| **Pet:** | A YORKSHIRE TERRIER |

## SAM JOHNSTONE

| | |
|---|---|
| **Team:** | EUXTON VILLA |
| **Replica shirt:** | MANCHESTER UNITED |
| **Game watched:** | I CAN'T REMEMBER! |
| **Album:** | NOW THAT'S WHAT I CALL MUSIC |
| **Pet:** | A RABBIT CALLED BUSTER |

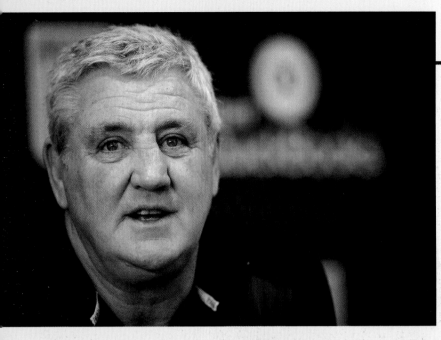

# MEET THE BOSS

Steve Bruce became the club's 28th manager when he took over last October after being appointed as successor to Roberto Di Matteo. Here are a few facts and figures about the man in charge of Villa's fortunes...

## OUR FRIEND FROM THE NORTH

The Villa boss was born Stephen Roger Bruce on 31st December 1960 in Corbridge, right in the heart of Hadrian's Wall country. An attractive tourist town, Corbridge is 16 miles west of Newcastle-on-Tyne. He grew up as a Newcastle United fan – and frequently crawled under the turnstiles at St James Park to avoid paying.

At the age of 13, while playing for the Newcastle Schools representative team, he was selected as a ball boy at for the 1974 League Cup final between Wolves and Manchester City at Wembley.

## BRUCE – OR BARNES?

Steve's talents are not restricted to football – he has also written three novels!

The books, written between 1999 and 2000, are called Sweeper, Striker and Defender. They are about Steve Barnes, the manager of fictional club Leddersfield Town – who solves crimes in his spare time.

## PLAYER OF THE YEAR

As a player, Steve was an uncompromising central defender. He began his career at Gillingham, making his debut in August 1979, and made such an impact over the following months that he was voted the Gills' Player of the Season. He played more than 200 games for the Kent club.

## OOPS! WRONG NET

Steve didn't have the best of starts to his time with Norwich City. On the opening day of the 1984-85 season he sent a powerful header flying into his own net to give champions Liverpool the lead at Carrow Road. The Canaries went 2-0 down and later trailed 3-2 but emerged from a thrilling game with a 3-3 draw.

## DOLLY AND DAISY

While he was with Manchester United, Steve formed a formidable defensive partnership with Gary Pallister. The pairing was later described on United's website as "probably the best in the club's history." The duo were affectionately known as Dolly and Daisy!

Steve won a host of honours at Old Trafford, including the Premier League title, the FA Cup (both three times), the League Cup and the European Cup Winners Cup when United beat Barcelona in the 1991 final.

## LUCKY SEVEN

Steve's first game as Villa manager was a 1-1 draw against Wolves at Villa Park last October. Three days later he led Villa to a 2-1 success at Reading — the team's first away win for 14 months, and they remained unbeaten for his first seven games in charge.

Sam Johnstone

**Do you know...**

# CONOR HOURIHANE?

**1** **In which country was Conor born?**

A Wales
B Ireland
C Scotland

**2** **From which club did he join Villa in last January's transfer window?**

A Barnsley
B Blackburn Rovers
C Bradford City

**3** **Villa also signed another player from the same club in January. Was it:**

A Scott Hogan?
B Henri Lansbury?
C James Bree?

**4** **Who were Villa's opponents when he made his debut?**

A Brentford
B Nottingham Forest
C Ipswich Town

**5** **Against which team did Conor score his first goal for Villa?**

A Derby County
B Bristol City
C Wigan Athletic

*Answers on page 61*

It's pretty much impossible to name the best line-up in the club's history because there are so many great players to choose from and everyone has a different opinion.

But we reckon this comes as close as anything, and our team doesn't even include pre-war greats like Pongo Waring, Eric Houghton and record scorer Billy Walker – simply because none of us saw them in action.

This team is based on submissions made by fans to the Villa News & Record throughout last season, with one vote awarded for each player's inclusion. Not surprisingly, the immaculate Paul McGrath was the most popular, with three members of Villa's European Cup-winning team – Gordon Cowans, Tony Morley and Dennis Mortimer – not far behind.

In addition to the 11 stars who make up this Villa Super Team, nominations were received for more than 60 other players, stretching back to the 1950s.

# THE SUPERMEN!

Goalkeeper
MARK BOSNICH
Villa years: 1992- 1999
228 appearances

Right-back
JOHN GIDMAN
Villa years: 1972-1979
243 appearances, 10 goals

Centre-back
PAUL McGRATH
Villa years: 1988-1996
323 appearances, 9 goals

Centre-back
MARTIN LAURSEN
Villa years 2004-2009
91 appearances, 11 goals

Left-back
STEVE STAUNTON
Villa years: 1991-1998 and
2000-2003
350 appearances, 20 goals

Right midfield
DENNIS MORTIMER
Villa years: 1975-1984
406 appearances, 36 goals

Centre midfield
GORDON COWANS
Villa years: 1976-1985 then
1988-1991 and 1993
527 appearances, 59 goals

Left midfield
TONY MORLEY
Villa years: 1979-1983
180 appearances, 34 goals

Striker
DAVID PLATT
Villa years: 1988-1991
155 appearances, 68 goals

Striker
PETER WITHE
Villa years: 1980-1985
233 appearances, 92 goals

BRIAN LITTLE
Villa years: 1971-1981
302 appearances, 82 goals

*Villa are right up there with the best when it comes to celebrities who are claret-and-blue through and through. Our famous fans come from the world of music, film, literature, politics and sport – and even the Royal Family!*

Nigel Kennedy – in tune with claret and blue.

# I'M A CELEBRITY...
# GET ME TO VILLA PARK!

### ROYALTY
HRH Prince William

### MUSIC
Nigel Kennedy
Stephen "Tin Tin" Duffy
Geezer Butler (Black Sabbath)
Roger Taylor (Duran Duran)
John Taylor (Duran Duran)

Phil Etheridge (The Twang)
Brian Travers (UB40)
Ritchie Neville (Five)
Kahn Morbee (The Parlatones)
Tom Tyler

### FILM
Tom Hanks
Oliver Phelps
David Bradley
Brendan Gleeson
Mark Williams

### TELEVISION
Helen George (Call the Midwife)
Nigel Boyle (Line of Duty)

**England cricketers Chris Woakes and Ian Bell relax in the Villa dressing room.**

Marc Baylis (Coronation Street)
Adil Ray (Citizen Khan)
Ian Lavender (Dad's Army)
Martin Shaw (Inspector George Gently)
Kris Marshall (Death in Paradise)
Pauline McLynn (Father Ted)

## RADIO

Phil Williams (BBC 5-Live presenter)

## SPORT

Ian Bell (Warwickshire and
England Cricket)
Chris Woakes (Warwickshire and
England Cricket)
Gianluca Pagliuca (former
Italy goalkeeper)
Katherine Merry (Athletics)
Tom Parsons (Athletics)
Dan Evans (Tennis)
Jane Sixsmith (Hockey)

Corrie's Marc Baylis.

## LITERATURE

Lee Child (Author)
Benjamin Zephania (Poet)

## POLITICS

David Cameron
Jacqui Smith
Lord Digby Jones

Lee Child with Villa legend Gordon Cowans.

# THE VILLA SQUAD

### SAM JOHNSTONE

**Born:** PRESTON,
25.03.93
**Position:** GOALKEEPER
**Signed:** JANUARY 2017 (loan)
**Previous club:** MANCHESTER UNITED
**Debut:** TOTTENHAM HOTSPUR (a)
08.01.17

### MARK BUNN

**Born:** LONDON,
16.11.84
**Position:** GOALKEEPER
**Signed:** JULY 2015
**Previous club:** NORWICH CITY
**Debut:** NOTTS COUNTY (h)
25.08.15

### JED STEER

**Born:** NORWICH,
23.09.92
**Position:** GOALKEEPER
**Signed:** JULY 2013
**Previous club:** NORWICH CITY
**Debut:** ROTHERHAM UNITED (h)
28.08.13

## JAMES BREE

| | |
|---|---|
| **Born:** | WAKEFIELD, 11.12.97 |
| **Position:** | FULL-BACK |
| **Signed:** | JANUARY 2017 |
| **Previous club:** | BARNSLEY |
| **Debut:** | NOTTINGHAM FOREST (a) 04.02.17 |

## KEINAN DAVIS

| | |
|---|---|
| **Born:** | STEVENAGE, 13.02.98 |
| **Position:** | STRIKER |
| **Joined Villa:** | DECEMBER 2015 |
| **Previous club:** | BIGGLESWADE TOWN |
| **Debut:** | TOTTENHAM HOTSPUR (a) 08.01.17 |

## NEIL TAYLOR

| | |
|---|---|
| **Born:** | ST ASAPH, WALES, 07.02.89 |
| **Position:** | FULL-BACK |
| **Signed:** | JANUARY 2017 |
| **Previous club:** | SWANSEA CITY |
| **Debut:** | IPSWICH TOWN (h) 11.04.17 |

## ALAN HUTTON

| | |
|---|---|
| **Born:** | GLASGOW, 30.11.84 |
| **Position:** | RIGHT-BACK |
| **Signed:** | AUGUST 2011 |
| **Previous club:** | TOTTENHAM |
| **Debut:** | EVERTON (a) 10.09.11 |

AHMED ELMOHAMADY

| | |
|---|---|
| **Born:** | BASYOUN, EGYPT, 09.09.87 |
| **Position:** | WINGER |
| **Joined Villa:** | JULY 2017 |
| **Previous club:** | HULL CITY |
| **Debut:** | HULL CITY (h) 05.08.17 |

## JOHN TERRY

| | |
|---|---|
| **Born:** | LONDON, 07.12.80 |
| **Position:** | CENTRAL DEFENDER |
| **Joined Villa:** | JULY 2017 |
| **Previous club:** | CHELSEA |
| **Debut:** | HULL CITY (h) 05.08.17 |

JACOB BEDEAU

| | |
|---|---|
| **Born:** | LONDON, 24.12.99 |
| **Position:** | FULL-BACK |
| **Signed:** | JANUARY 2017 |
| **Previous club:** | BURY |

## JAMES CHESTER

| | |
|---|---|
| **Born:** | WARRINGTON, 23.01.89 |
| **Position:** | CENTRE-BACK |
| **Signed:** | AUGUST 2016 |
| **Previous club:** | WEST BROMWICH ALBION |
| **Debut:** | ROTHERHAM UNITED (h) 13.08.16 |

TOMMY ELPHICK

| | |
|---|---|
| **Born:** | BRIGHTON, 07.09.87 |
| **Position:** | CENTRE-BACK |
| **Signed:** | JUNE 2016 |
| **Previous club:** | BOURNEMOUTH |
| **Debut:** | SHEFFIELD WEDNESDAY (a) 07.08.16 |

### CHRIS SAMBA

| | |
|---|---|
| **Born:** | CRETEIL, FRANCE, 28.03.84 |
| **Position:** | CENTRAL DEFENDER |
| **Joined Villa:** | JULY 2017 |
| **Previous club:** | PANATHANAIKOS |
| **Debut:** | HULL CITY (h) 05.08.17 |

### MICAH RICHARDS

| | |
|---|---|
| **Born:** | BIRMINGHAM, 24.06.88 |
| **Position:** | DEFENDER |
| **Signed:** | JUNE 2015 |
| **Previous club:** | MANCHESTER CITY |
| **Debut:** | BOURNEMOUTH (a) 08.08.15 |

### GARY GARDNER

| | |
|---|---|
| **Born:** | SOLIHUILL, 26.02.92 |
| **Position:** | MIDFIELDER |
| **Signed:** | ACADEMY GRADUATE |
| **Debut:** | CHELSEA (a) 31.12.11 |

### JAKE DOYLE-HAYES

| | |
|---|---|
| **Born:** | DUBLIN, 30.12.98 |
| **Position:** | MIDFIELDER |
| **Joined Villa:** | ACADEMY GRADUATE |
| **Debut:** | WIGAN ATHLETIC (h) 22.08.17 |

### GLENN WHELAN

| | |
|---|---|
| **Born:** | CLONDALKIN, IRELAND, 13.01.84 |
| **Position:** | MIDFIELDER |
| **Joined Villa:** | JULY 2017 |
| **Previous club:** | STOKE CITY |
| **Debut:** | HULL CITY (h) 05.08.17 |

## SCOTT HOGAN

| | |
|---|---|
| **Born:** | SALFORD, |
| | 13.04.92 |
| **Position:** | STRIKER |
| **Signed:** | JANUARY 2017 |
| **Previous club:** | BRENTFORD |
| **Debut:** | NOTTINGHAM FOREST (a) |
| | 04.02.17 |

## GABBY AGBONLAHOR

| | |
|---|---|
| **Born:** | BIRMINGHAM, |
| | 13.10.86 |
| **Position:** | STRIKER |
| **Signed:** | ACADEMY GRADUATE |
| **Debut:** | EVERTON (a) |
| | 18.03.06 |

## JACK GREALISH

| | |
|---|---|
| **Born:** | BIRMINGHAM, |
| | 10.09.95 |
| **Position:** | MIDFIELDER |
| **Signed:** | ACADEMY GRADUATE |
| **Debut:** | MANCHESTER CITY (a) |
| | 07.05.14 |

## CONOR HOURIHANE

| | |
|---|---|
| **Born:** | BANDON, IRELAND, |
| | 02.02.91 |
| **Position:** | MIDFIELDER |
| **Signed:** | JANUARY 2017 |
| **Previous club:** | BARNSLEY |
| **Debut:** | BRENTFORD (a) |
| | 31.01.17 |

## BIRKIR BJARNASON

| | |
|---|---|
| **Born:** | AKUREYRI, ICELAND, |
| | 27.05.88 |
| **Position:** | MIDFIELDER |
| **Signed:** | JANUARY 2017 |
| **Previous club:** | BASEL |
| **Debut:** | BRENTFORD (a) |
| | 31.01.17 |

## HENRI LANSBURY

| | |
|---|---|
| **Born:** | LONDON, 12.10.90 |
| **Position:** | MIDFIELDER |
| **Signed:** | JANUARY 2017 |
| **Previous club:** | NOTTINGHAM FOREST |
| **Debut:** | PRESTON (h) 21.01.17 |

## ROBERT SNODGRASS

| | |
|---|---|
| **Born:** | GLASGOW, 07.09.87 |
| **Position:** | WINGER |
| **Joined Villa:** | AUGUST 2017 |
| **Previous club:** | WEST HAM UNITED |

## CALLUM O'HARE

| | |
|---|---|
| **Born:** | SOLIHULL, 01.05.98 |
| **Position:** | MIDFIELDER |
| **Joined Villa:** | ACADEMY GRADUATE |
| **Debut:** | COLCHESTER UNITED (a) 09.08.17 |

## KEVIN TONER

| | |
|---|---|
| **Born:** | DUBLIN, 18.06.96 |
| **Position:** | DEFENDER |
| **Signed:** | ACADEMY GRADUATE |
| **Debut:** | SOUTHAMPTON (h) 23.04.16 |

## JOSH ONOMAH

| | |
|---|---|
| **Born:** | LONDON, 27.04.97 |
| **Position:** | MIDFIELDER |
| **Joined Villa:** | AUGUST 2017 |
| **Previous club:** | TOTTENHAM HOTSPUR |
| **Debut:** | HULL CITY (h) 05.08.17 |

### JORDAN LYDEN

| | |
|---|---|
| **Born:** | PERTH, AUSTRALIA, 30.01.96 |
| **Position:** | MIDFIELDER |
| **Signed:** | ACADEMY GRADUATE |
| **Debut:** | WYCOMBE WANDERERS (a) 09.01.16 |

### ROSS McCORMACK

| | |
|---|---|
| **Born:** | GLASGOW, 18.08.86 |
| **Position:** | STRIKER |
| **Signed:** | AUGUST 2016 |
| **Previous club:** | FULHAM |
| **Debut:** | SHEFFIELD WEDNESDAY (a) 07.08.16 |

### MILE JEDINAK

| | |
|---|---|
| **Born:** | SYDNEY, AUSTRALIA, 03.08.84 |
| **Position:** | MIDFIELDER |
| **Signed:** | AUGUST 2016 |
| **Previous club:** | CRYSTAL PALACE |
| **Debut:** | BRISTOL CITY (a) 27.08.16 |

### RITCHIE DE LAET

| | |
|---|---|
| **Born:** | ANTWERP, BELGIUM, 28.11.88 |
| **Position:** | DEFENDER |
| **Signed:** | AUGUST 2016 |
| **Previous club:** | LEICESTER CITY |
| **Debut:** | BRISTOL CITY (a) 27.08.16 |

## ANDRE GREEN

**Born:** SOLIHULL, 26.07.98
**Position:** MIDFIELDER
**Signed:** ACADEMY GRADUATE
**Debut:** TOTTENHAM HOTSPUR (h) 13.03.16

## RUSHIAN HEPBURN-MURPHY

**Born:** BIRMINGHAM, 28.08.98
**Position:** STRIKER
**Joined Villa:** ACADEMY GRADUATE
**Debut:** SUNDERLAND (h) 14.03.15

## JONATHAN KODJIA

**Born:** PARIS, 22.10.89
**Position:** STRIKER
**Joined Villa:** AUGUST 2016
**Previous club:** BRISTOL CITY
**Debut:** NOTTINGHAM FOREST (h) 11.09.16

## ALBERT ADOMAH

**Born:** LONDON, 13.12.87
**Position:** MIDFIELDER
**Joined Villa:** AUGUST 2016
**Previous club:** MIDDLESBROUGH
**Debut:** IPSWICH TOWN (a) 17.09.16

# THE FIRST GOALS CLUB...

## 1 JACK GREALISH
**(Rotherham United home, 13th August 2016) 3-0**

Scoring your first goal for a club is always a special occasion, and 10 Villa players experienced that particular thrill last season. Although Jack Grealish had scored at Leicester the previous year, we have included the special moment he netted his first goal at Villa Park.

## 2 ROSS McCORMACK
**(Huddersfield Town home, 16th August 2016) 1-1**

Our summer signing from Fulham headed in from close range after Jack Grealish had hooked Leandro Bacuna's deep centre back across the face of the goal.

## 3 JONATHAN KODJIA
**(Brentford home, 14th September 2016) 1-1**

Accepting a pass from Mile Jedinak, the former Bristol City striker cut inside from the right before drilling a perfect rising left-foot shot into the far corner.

## 4 AARON TSHIBOLA
**(Newcastle United home, 24th September 2016) 1-1**

With Villa facing defeat, the former Reading midfielder rose at the far post to meet Jordan Ayew's left-wing corner and squeeze a header past keeper Matz Sels.

## 5 GARY GARDNER

**(Birmingham City away, 30th October 2016) 1-1**
Gary raced almost the full length of the pitch to celebrate with the claret-and-blue faithful after his looping header had given Villa a 29th-minute lead in the Second City derby.

## 6 NATHAN BAKER

**(Brighton & Hove Albion away, 18th November 2016) 1-1**
Nearly six years after making his debut, the central defender finally scored his first goal with a fine header from Albert Adomah's free-kick at the Amex Stadium.

## 7 ALBERT ADOMAH

**(Cardiff City home, 26th November 2016) 1-1**
The winger was a picture of composure as he controlled Jordan Amavi's low cross from the left before firing home firmly at the far post.

## 8 JAMES CHESTER

**(Derby County home, 25th February 2017) 1-0**
The central defender flicked the ball up with his knee and headed in from close range after Jonathan Kodjia had helped on Henri Lansbury's corner.

## 9 CONOR HOURIHANE

**(Bristol City home, 28th February 2017) 2-0**
Albert Adomah miskicked after being set up by Jonathan Kodjia's pass, but Hourihane was well positioned to drill home a low right-foot shot.

## 10 SCOTT HOGAN

**(Wigan Athletic away, 18th March 2017) 2-0**
Back in the side after a five-match injury absence, Hogan headed home firmly from Albert Adomah's 84th-minute cross to seal Villa's fifth win in six games.

Conor Hourihane

James Chester was Villa's skipper for most of last season. Can you name 12 other players who have been Villa captains down the years, using the initials of Chester's name and the clues provided below?

# Name the captains

*Answers on page 61*

**Crossword grid (filled in):**

- J a s z c z u n
- J (ONIB) B a r r y
- A S c h m e i c h e l
- M e l l b e r g
- T o w n s e n d
- R i o c h
- S o u t h g a t e
- P e t r o v
- L a u r s e n
- S t a u n t o n
- B e n t
- R i c h a r d s o n

---

**1 TOMMY J**
This youngster with a Polish surname played just once for the first team but was captain for two pre-season friendlies in 1999.

**2 GARETH B**
An England international who played in defence or midfield

**3 PETER S**
Danish keeper who is Villa's oldest scorer!

**4 OLOF M**
Swedish defender who excelled between 2001 and 2008.

**5 ANDY T**
Midfielder who lifted the League Cup in 1996.

**6 BRUCE R**
An English-born Scotland international.

**7 GARETH S**
Villa's captain in the 2000 FA Cup final.

**8 STILIYAN P**
Bulgarian midfielder who was forced to retire through illness.

**9 MARTIN L**
Classy Danish defender who arrived from Milan.

**10 STEVE S**
Versatile Irishman who had two spells with both Villa and Liverpool.

**11 DARREN B**
Villa's record signing was briefly skipper in 2012.

**12 KEVIN R**
Captained Villa to victory over Man United in the 1994 League Cup final.

# WHO WEARS THE SHIRT?

**Answers on page 60**

Something has gone wrong with the names on these Villa shirts. But if you rearrange the letters you will discover the names of 12 Villa players.

RETRY
**1**
Terry

TORY AL
**2**
Taylor

ETCHERS
**3**
Chester

I OKD AJ
**4**
Kodjia

OH NAG
**5**
Hogan

AH, HERO IN U
**6**
Hourihane

SON BANJAR
**7**
Bjarnason

ELATED
**8**
Delaet

HO ADAM
**9**
Adomah

DIVAS
**10**
Davis

OH NO BAR GAL
**11**
Agbonlahor

BANS RULY
**12**
Lansbury

# SPOT THE DIFFERENCE

Can you spot the ten differences in this image of our team training?

*Answers on page 6*

1, 2, 3, 4, 5, 6, 7, 8, 9, 10

# GOING UP...

*Debut boy Stuart Gray leaps into action against Bradford City at Valley Parade.*

*Garry Thompson celebrates with Villa fans after the final game at Swindon.*

Everyone connected with Villa has the same ambition – to see our famous old club back in the Premier League. And how fitting it would be if that were to happen in 2018. It's 30 years since Villa were last promoted to English football's top flight – then known as the First Division. The club had been relegated

Sports Argus

**WE'RE UP**

PROMOTION SPECIAL  25p

*The Sports Argus produced a special edition to mark Villa's promotion.*

won just once, and could do little right at Villa Park. But things slowly improved and the real turning point came in November. Scottish striker Alan McInally scored his first league goal for the club to secure a 1-0 win at Oldham, and the following Saturday new signing Stuart Gray netted twice in a 4-2 win at Bradford City.

Those wins started a run of 12 games without defeat, and promotion was finally clinched on the final day. Villa drew 0-0 away to Swindon Town but results elsewhere meant they were promoted by the narrowest of margins.

Their goal difference of 27 was exactly the same as third-placed Middlesbrough but Villa went up automatically because they had scored more goals than the Teessiders, who were eventually promoted via the play-offs.

the previous season but the appointment of Graham Taylor in the summer of 1987 was a major coup.

Taylor, who sadly died last January, was one of the most successful managers in the game, having guided Watford from the Fourth Division to the First.

He immediately began the task of rebuilding the Villa team, although it was tough initially. After seven games, Villa had

**Graham Taylor, Manager, 1987.**

## TOP OF THE TABLE

|  | P | W | D | L | F | A | Pts |
|---|---|---|---|---|---|---|---|
| Millwall | 44 | 25 | 7 | 12 | 72 | 52 | 82 |
| **Villa** | **44** | **22** | **12** | **10** | **68** | **41** | **78** |
| Middlesbrough | 44 | 22 | 12 | 10 | 63 | 36 | 78 |
| Bradford City | 44 | 22 | 11 | 11 | 74 | 54 | 77 |
| Blackburn Rovers | 44 | 21 | 14 | 9 | 68 | 52 | 77 |

## AUGUST

We've been warned that life in the Championship is tough, and the first month of the season underlines the point.

After slipping to a late goal on the opening day at Hillsborough, Villa crash out of the EFL Cup at Kenilworth Road, going down 3-1 to League Two outfit Luton Town after going in front through Jordan Ayew.

The first home match brings a welcome boost, Rudy Gestede netting twice against Rotherham United before Jack Grealish seals a 3-0 victory by waltzing through the visitors' defence for his first Villa goal.

A Ross McCormack header gives Villa the lead against Huddersfield Town, only for the Yorkshire side to grab a late equaliser. And although a goalless draw at Derby is a decent result, the month ends with a defeat to Bristol City after Jack Grealish's superb volley opens the scoring at Ashton Gate.

### Results

| | | | |
|---|---|---|---|
| Aug 7 | SHEFFIELD WEDNESDAY | A 0-1 | |
| Aug 10 | LUTON TOWN (EFL Cup) | A 1-3 | Ayew |
| Aug 13 | ROTHERHAM UNITED | H 3-0 | Gestede 2, Grealish |
| Aug 16 | HUDDERSFIELD TOWN | H 1-1 | McCormack |
| Aug 20 | DERBY COUNTY | A 0-0 | |
| Aug 27 | BRISTOL CITY | A 1-3 | Grealish |

## SEPTEMBER

Villa become the country's draw specialists, taking a single point from each of their five games during September.

Trailing to Nottingham Forest, the boys in claret and blue storm ahead with goals from Ross McCormack and Rudy Gestede in the space of three minutes, only for Henri Lansbury to equalise in the 87th minute.

And although Jonathan Kodjia scores his first goal for the club four days later, there's more late anguish as John Egan equalises for Brentford on 88 minutes.

After a goalless encounter at Ipswich, it's Villa's turn to score late, Aaron Tshibola's header earning a draw against leaders Newcastle. But there's more frustration at Barnsley, where Sam Winnall's last-gasp header cancels out Jordan Ayew's opening goal.

### Results

| | | | | |
|---|---|---|---|---|
| Sept 11 | NOTTINGHAM FOREST | H | 2-2 | McCormack, Gestede |
| Sept 14 | BRENTFORD | H | 1-1 | Kodjia |
| Sept 17 | IPSWICH TOWN | A | 0-0 | |
| Sept 24 | NEWCASTLE UNITED | H | 1-1 | Tshibola |
| Sept 27 | BARNSLEY | A | 1-1 | Ayew |

# OCTOBER

Steve Bruce takes over as manager following a defeat at Preston and the new boss has an immediate impact.

In Bruce's first game in charge, Jonathan Kodjia's penalty against Wolves is nullified by Helder Costa's spot kick but four days later Villa record their first away win of the season.

Although Kodjia's first-half goal is cancelled out by Yann Kermorgant, a dramatic finale sees sub Jordan Ayew convert a last-minute penalty to the delight of 4,000 travelling fans.

Kodjia's spectacular 80th minute volley – his

third goal in as many games – secures a narrow home victory for Fulham before Gary Gardner scores his first Villa goal in the Second City derby at St Andrew's.

### Results

| | | | | |
|---|---|---|---|---|
| Oct 1 | PRESTON NORTH END | A | 0-2 | |
| Oct 15 | WOLVES | H | 1-1 | Kodjia pen |
| Oct 18 | READING | A | 2-1 | Kodjia, Ayew pen |
| Oct 22 | FULHAM | H | 1-0 | Kodjia |
| Oct 30 | BIRMINGHAM CITY | A | 1-1 | Gardner |

# NOVEMBER

Villa comebacks have been rare over the past few years but Bruce's boys display their fighting spirit after trailing to Blackburn Rovers at Villa Park.

Jonathan Kodjia brings the scores level with a 58th minute penalty after Jack Grealish is brought down in the area, and the Ivory Coast international slots home his second on 70 minutes following a magnificent pass from Mile Jedinak.

Defender Nathan Baker becomes the latest player to claim his first Villa goal, heading the visitors into the lead against second-placed Brighton & Hove Albion.

And although Villa have to settle for a point at the Amex Stadium, the month ends on a high with victory over Cardiff City. This time Albert Adomah is the man scoring his first goal for the club, with a Kodjia header and a late penalty from sub Rudy Gestede securing three points.

## Results

| Nov 5 | BLACKBURN ROVERS | H | 2-1 | Kodjia 2 |
| Nov 18 | BRIGHTON | A | 1-1 | Baker |
| Nov 26 | CARDIFF CITY | H | 3-1 | Adomah, Kodjia, Gestede pen |

# DECEMBER

A 2-0 setback at Leeds is Villa's first defeat under Steve Bruce's management, and the team also slip to a 1-0 defeat at Norwich City.

But sandwiched between those two disappointments, Jack Grealish's superb late goal clinches a 1-0 home win over Wigan Athletic, and the festive season is also a productive period.

A Jonathan Kodjia goal is enough to secure three points against Queens Park Rangers at Loftus Road, while the historic first-ever competitive game between Villa and Burton Albion attracts a bumper Boxing Day crowd of 41,337.

Leandro Bacuna opens the scoring against the Brewers with a powerful header, only for former Villa youngster Jamie Ward to equalise with a fine volley. But Ross McCormack secures maximum points with a 78th minute winner.

Three nights later, Kodjia's late penalty earns a 1-1 draw with high-riding Leeds in an exciting contest.

## Results

| Dec 3 | LEEDS UNITED | A | 0-2 | |
| Dec 10 | WIGAN ATHLETIC | H | 1-0 | Grealish |
| Dec 13 | NORWICH CITY | A | 0-1 | |
| Dec 18 | QUEENS PARK RANGERS | A | 1-0 | Kodjia |
| Dec 26 | BURTON ALBION | H | 2-1 | Bacuna, McCormack |
| Dec 29 | LEEDS UNITED | H | 1-1 | Kodjia pen |

## JANUARY/FEBRUARY

Despite a lot of transfer activity, with eight new players coming in and the same number leaving, January is a disappointing month on the pitch, Villa's only point coming in a 2-2 home draw against Preston – after leading 2-0 through Albert Adomah's first-half brace.

The team also suffer four straight defeats in February before getting back on track with back-to-back victories against Derby County and Bristol City.

James Chester scores his first goal for the club with a close-range header which secures victory over the Rams and four days later Hourihane also claims his first goal in claret and blue, firing home a low shot against the Robins after Jonathan Kodjia opens the scoring against his former club with a fine glancing header.

Unfortunately the win against Derby is marred by the sending-off of Leandro Bacuna, who angrily confronts a linesman in stoppage time.

| | | | | |
|---|---|---|---|---|
| Jan 2 | CARDIFF CITY | A | 0-1 | |
| Jan 8 | TOTTENHAM (FAC 3) | A | 0-2 | |
| Jan 14 | WOLVES | A | 0-1 | |
| Jan 21 | PRESTON NORTH END | H | 2-2 | Adomah 2 |
| Jan 31 | BRENTFORD | H | 0-3 | |
| Feb 4 | NOTTINGHAM FOREST | A | 1-2 | Kodjia |
| Feb 11 | IPSWICH TOWN | H | 0-1 | |
| Feb 14 | BARNSLEY | H | 1-3 | Kodjia |
| Feb 20 | NEWCASTLE UNITED | A | 0-2 | |
| Feb 25 | DERBY COUNTY | H | 1-0 | Chester |
| Feb 28 | BRISTOL CITY | H | 2-0 | Kodjia, Hourihane |

## MARCH

Already hit by a number of injuries, Villa receive a further blow when Leandro Bacuna is suspended for six matches for his red card against Derby.

Twenty-four hours after the ban is announced by the FA, Villa record a third consecutive victory, emerging 2-0 winners over bottom-of-the-table Rotherham United at the New York Stadium. After a goalless first half, Steve Bruce's side go ahead through a Will Vaulks own goal before Jonathan Kodjia's low shot secures all three points. The winning sequence comes to an end in a 1-0 defeat at Huddersfield Town but Villa bounce back with a 2-0 home success over Sheffield Wednesday, Kodjia netting both goals to take his haul for the season to 15.

Scott Hogan returns from injury for the visit to Wigan – and scores his first Villa goal with a firm header from Albert Adomah's right-wing cross. The goal clinches three points after James Chester heads the visitors in front at the DW Stadium.

| Mar 4 | ROTHERHAM UNITED | A 2-0 | Vaulks og, Kodjia |
| Mar 7 | HUDDERSFIELD TOWN | A 0-1 | |
| Mar 11 | SHEFFIELD WEDNESDAY | H 2-0 | Kodjia 2 |
| Mar 18 | WIGAN ATHLETIC | A 2-0 | Chester, Hogan |

## APRIL/MAY

Victories over Norwich and QPR in the space of a few days extend Villa's winning run to four games – the club's best sequence since December 2009. Jonathan Kodjia is on target twice against the Canaries and also scores the winner against Rangers, but his goal against Burton Albion the following Saturday isn't enough to prevent a 1-1 draw which ends Villa's slender hopes of making the Championship play-offs. That's followed by a home defeat by Reading on the weekend Villa Park celebrates its 120th anniversary and an Easter Monday setback by the same margin at

the hands of Fulham, despite a superb equaliser from Jack Grealish. To add to the misery, Kodjia is sent off at Craven Cottage.

But the Second City derby produces a sensational story. Gabby Agbonlahor, sidelined by injury for three months and without a goal since February 2016, goes on as a substitute for Grealish in the 59th minute – and scores the winner nine minutes later.

After a narrow defeat at Blackburn, the season ends on a high note as Grealish's late equaliser earns a 1-1 home draw against promoted Brighton & Hove Albion.

## Results

| April 1 | NORWICH CITY | H | 2-0 | Kodjia 2 |
| April 4 | QUEENS PARK RANGERS | H | 1-0 | Kodjia |
| April 8 | BURTON ALBION | A | 1-1 | Kodjia |
| April 15 | READING | H | 1-3 | Chester |
| April 17 | FULHAM | A | 1-3 | Grealish |
| April 23 | BIRMINGHAM CITY | H | 1-0 | Agbonlahor |
| April 29 | BLACKBURN ROVERS | A | 0-1 | |
| May 7 | BRIGHTON | H | 1-1 | Grealish |

Birkir Bjarnason

# DEBUTS 2016-17

PIERLUIGI GOLLINI v SHEFFIELD WEDNESDAY (A)

TOMMY ELPHICK v SHEFFIELD WEDNESDAY (A)

ROSS McCORMACK v SHEFFIELD WEDNESDAY (A)

AARON TSHIBOLA v SHEFFIELD WEDNESDAY (A)

JAMES CHESTER v ROTHERHAM UNITED (H)

MILE JEDINAK v BRISTOL CITY (A)

RITCHIE DE LAET v BRISTOL CITY (A)

JONATHAN KODJIA v NOTTINGHAM FOREST (H)

ALBERT ADOMAH v IPSWICH TOWN (A)

SAM JOHNSTONE v TOTTENHAM HOTSPUR (A)

KEINAN DAVIS v TOTTENHAM HOTSPUR (A)

HENRI LANSBURY v PRESTON NORTH END (H)

CONOR HOURIHANE v BRENTFORD (A)

BIRKIR BJARNASON v BRENTFORD (A)

JAMES BREE v NOTTINGHAM FOREST (A)

SCOTT HOGAN v NOTTINGHAM FOREST (A)

NEIL TAYLOR v IPSWICH TOWN (H)

COREY BLACKETT-TAYLOR v HUDDERSFIELD TOWN (A)

## STAT ATTACK

# APPEARANCES AND GOALS 2016-17

**1 PIERLUIGI GOLLINI**
A 20 league

**2 NATHAN BAKER**
A 31(1) league, 2 cup
G 1 league

**3 NEIL TAYLOR**
A 14 league

**4 MICAH RICHARDS**
A 1(1) league, 1 cup

**5 HENRI LANSBURY**
A 17(1) league

**5* JORES OKORE**
A 1 cup

**6 TOMMY ELPHICK**
A 20(6) league

**7 LEANDRO BACUNA**
A 22(8) league, 1 cup
G 1 league

**8 AARON TSHIBOLA**
A 5(3) league, 2 cup
G 1 league

**9 SCOTT HOGAN**
A 9(4) league
G 1 league

**10 JORDAN AYEW**
A 14(4) league, 1 cup
G 2 league, 1 cup

**11 GABBY AGBONLAHOR**
A 4(9) league, 1 cup
G 1 league

**12 JAMES CHESTER**
A 45 league, 1 cup
G 3 league

**14 CONOR HOURIHANE**
A 13(4) league
G 1 league

**14* RUDY GESTEDE**
A 8(10) league, 0(1) cup
G 4 league

**15 ASHLEY WESTWOOD**
A 18(5) league

**16 JAMES BREE**
A 6(1) league

**18 LIBOR KOZAK**
A 0(2) league

**19 ANDRE GREEN**
A 4(11) league, 1(1) cup

**20 BIRKIR BJARNASON**
A 5(3) league

**20* ADAMA TRAORE**
A 0(1) league

**21 ALAN HUTTON**
A 31(3) league, 1(1) cup

**22 GARY GARDNER**
A 18(8) league, 1 cup
G 1 league

**23 JORDAN AMAVI**
A 26(8) league, 2 cup

**25 MILE JEDINAK**
A 33 league, 1 cup

**26 JONATHAN KODJIA**
A 36 league
G 19 league

**27 RITCHIE DE LAET**
A 3 league

**28 ALY CISSOKHO**
A 11(1) league

**29 RUSHIAN HEPBURN-MURPHY**
A 0(3) league

**31 MARK BUNN**
A 5(1) league, 1 cup

**34 SAM JOHNSTONE**
A 21 league, 1 cup

**35 COREY BLACKETT-TAYLOR**
A 0(1) league

**37 ALBERT ADOMAH**
A 30(8) league, 1 cup
G 3 league

**39 KEINAN DAVIS**
A 0(6) league, 0(1) cup

**44 ROSS McCORMACK**
A 17(7) league, 1(1) cup
G 3 league

**KEY**
*A* **APPEARANCES**
*G* **GOALS**
*(1)* **SUB APPEARANCES**
*\* Two players wore shirt numbers 5, 14 and 20*

# OPENING THE WINDOW

It will be interesting to see which players Villa sign or sell during the first month of the New Year, but surely there will never be another January transfer window to match the first 31 days of 2017?

It was a truly amazing month at Villa Park as the club signed EIGHT new players – seven on a permanent basis plus keeper Sam Johnstone on loan.

And during the same hectic period, eight players also left the club, including five who made loan moves. This is how the window unfolded down Witton way…

## ⬈ IN

**SAM JOHNSTONE** (Manchester United) *

**HENRI LANSBURY** (Nottingham Forest)

**CONOR HOURIHANE** (Barnsley)

**JAMES BREE** (Barnsley)

**BIRKIR BJARNASON** (Basel)

**NEIL TAYLOR** (Swansea City)

**SCOTT HOGAN** (Brentford)

**JACOB BEDEAU** (Bury)

## ⬋ OUT

**RUDY GESTEDE** (Middlesbrough)

**ASHLEY WESTWOOD** (Burnley)

**JORDAN AYEW** (Swansea City)

**ROSS McCORMACK** (Nottingham Forest) *

**AARON TSHIBOLA** (Nottingham Forest) *

**PIERLUIGI GOLLINI** (Atalanta) *

**ALY CISSOKHO** (Olympiacos) *

**KEVIN TONER** (Bradford City) *

*\* Loan deals*

John Terry

# PLAYERS AND PLACES...

**Various Villa players down the years have shared their names with towns, cities and even countries.**

**Here's a selection of Villans whose names might just help you with your geography lessons!**

## JAMES CHESTER

Central defender who joined Villa from West Brom in the summer of 2016 after some impressive displays for Wales at the World Cup finals in France.

### CHESTER

A city in north-west England which was founded in the 1st century AD. It is famous for its well-preserved Roman walls.

## DION DUBLIN

This striker scored seven goals in his first three Villa games – a club record – after signing from Coventry City in November 1998.

### DUBLIN

The capital of the Republic of Ireland, this popular city lies at the mouth of the River Liffey.

## STEPHEN IRELAND

A midfielder who joined Villa from Manchester City when James Milner moved in the other direction in 2010.

### IRELAND

Otherwise known as Eire, the Republic of Ireland is actually the country where Stephen Ireland was born!

## MARC ALBRIGHTON

A Villa-supporting winger who had the thrill of playing for his favourite team before moving to Leicester City. Marc had the distinction of scoring the Premier League's 20,000th goal when he netted against Arsenal in 2011.

### ALBRIGHTON

A large village in Shropshire, almost seven miles west of Wolverhampton. One of its main attractions is the RAF Museum at nearby Cosford.

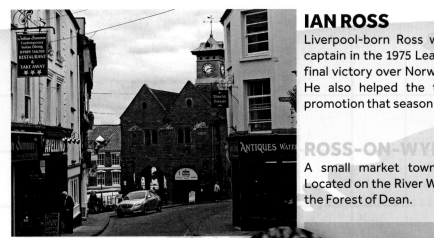

## IAN ROSS

Liverpool-born Ross was Villa's captain in the 1975 League Cup final victory over Norwich City. He also helped the team to promotion that season.

### ROSS-ON-WYE

A small market town in south-east Herefordshire. Located on the River Wye, it is on the northern edge of the Forest of Dean.

## FERNANDO NELSON

This Portuguese right-back played 73 league and cup games during two successful seasons at Villa Park after signing from Sporting Lisbon in 1996.

### NELSON

A small Lancashire town which lies four miles north of Burnley, on the Leeds and Liverpool Canal.

## TOMMY WESTON

Not many players can claim to have won FA Cup medals either side of a world war, but Tommy did. An accomplished full-back, he helped Villa to Cup glory in 1913 and again in 1920.

### WESTON-SUPER-MARE

A seaside resort in the south west, which is hugely popular with holiday-makers and day-trippers from the Midlands. It is famous for its Grand Pier – and donkey rides on the beach!

## MATHIEU BERSON

A French midfielder who played just 13 games for Villa following his move from Nantes in 2004. He subsequently joined Spanish club Levante.

### BERSON

A commune near the town of Blaye in the Gironde department of south-west France – an area renowned for its Bordeaux wine.

# WHEN WAS THIS?

Can you name the year in which these momentous claret-and-blue events happened?

*Answers on page 61*

**1** The Duke of Edinburgh is introduced to the Villa team before the FA Cup final against Manchester United at Wembley.

(a) 1957 ✓

(b) 1958

(c) 1959

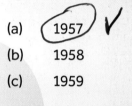

**2** Villa's players line up for a team photo after becoming the first winners of the League Cup.

(a) 1960

(b) 1961 ✓

(c) 1963

**3** Skipper Bruce Rioch proudly displays the trophy at Villa Park after Villa clinch promotion from the old Third Division.

(a) 1971

(b) 1972 ✓

(c) 1975

**4** Dalian Atkinson celebrates with "Rain Man" after scoring what was voted BBC's Goal of the Season.

(a) 1990

(b) 1991

(c) 1992 ✓

## FIVE-STAR SHOWS!

**Harry Hampton**

Villa had been in existence for the best part of four decades before one of our players scored five goals in a single game – and then it happened in two consecutive home matches!

Harry Hampton, the club's record league scorer, was the first Villan to achieve the feat when he netted five times in a 10-0 thrashing of Sheffield Wednesday on Saturday 5th October 1912.

Two weeks later, with Hampton ruled out by an injury, Harold Halse repeated the feat by scoring all five goals in a 5-1 victory over Derby County.

*Only three other Villa players have scored five goals in one game –*

>> **Len Capewell** in a 10-0 win against Burnley on the opening day of the 1925-26 season.

>> **George Brown** in an 8-3 success at Leicester City in 1932.

>> **Gerry Hitchens** in an 11-1 victory over Charlton Athletic in November 1959.

## SIGNING OFF IN STYLE

Frank Carrodus wasn't what you would describe as a prolific marksman for Villa, the midfielder scoring just seven times in 151 league games for the club.

But he clearly liked to save his goals for the final day of the season. He was on target against Norwich City in 1975, Middlesbrough in 1976 and Wolves in 1978.

## DAY OF THE DOUBLE

Villa are one of only seven clubs to achieve a league and FA Cup double, along with Manchester United, Arsenal, Chelsea, Liverpool, Tottenham Hotspur and Preston North End, who were the very first double winners in 1889.

**Gerry Hitchens**

But Villa's double is unique – we became champions and Cup winners on the same day!

On Saturday 10th April 1897, the boys in claret and blue beat Everton in the Cup Final at Crystal Palace – and then discovered they had also won the title because Derby County, the only team who could have caught them, had lost to Bury.

# Glenn Whelan

# SPOT THE BALL

**Can you spot which one is the real ball?**

*Answers on page 60*

# THE CUBS

## ROAR WITH THE LION CUBS!

**THE CUBS ARE READY TO ROAR – AND YOU CAN ROAR WITH THEM.**

Young supporters have always been important to Villa, and that's truer than ever following a major revamp of our junior section.

It started as the Little Villans and then became JV-Life. Now the junior club has been rebranded simply THE CUBS.

One of Villa's central aims is to welcome families and bring young lions closer to the club – we're very much a pride of lions!

That's where The Cubs comes in. Membership is **FREE** to all junior season ticket holders and offers members some great benefits throughout the year.

**THESE INCLUDE:**

**WELCOME PACK**
WITH EXCLUSIVE PIN BADGE
**& VERY SPECIAL HOODY** OR
**JACKET** THAT YOU WON'T
FIND ANYWHERE ELSE!*

Access to
PRIDE REWARDS

**INVITES TO EVENTS**

**EXCLUSIVE COMPETITIONS**

**CHANCE TO BE A MASCOT**

**BIRTHDAY CARD & CHRISTMAS CARD**

## ...plus much, much more!

*Additional fee applies for Season Ticket Holders

ARE YOU
# PART OF THE PRIDE?

There are also plenty of other opportunities to be closer to the club. Mascots Hercules, Bella and Chip will be on hand at the many other events held at Villa Park, with a firm focus on welcoming new families.

This is epitomised by the regular Family Fun Zone on match days, an area which continues to grow and improve with the help of supporters' feedback.

And even for those youngsters who are not junior season ticket holders, the cost for all of this is just £20 a year!

To enroll just call 0333 323 1874 or go to www.avfc.co.uk/membership.

## SO YOU WANT TO BE A MASCOT?

Being a full member of The Cubs means you will have the chance to be a match-day mascot – an unforgettable experience for any young supporter.

If you are lucky enough to be randomly selected, you will get the chance to display your skills on the pitch before kick-off, sit in the home dug-out, walk out with the players and line-up for the handshakes with the opposition.

You will also receive a souvenir photo of your big day.

# IT FIGURES ...

**Significant numbers which have shaped Villa's history.**

## 7

The number of times we have won the League Championship (and also the FA Cup).

## 49

Tom "Pongo" Waring's record number of league goals in one season, 1930-31 (and he also scored one in the FA Cup!)

## 1961

The year that Villa won the inaugural League Cup competition.

## 660

Full-back Charlie Aitken's club record appearances between 1961 and 1976.

## 244

Billy Walker's club record league and cup goals from 1921 to 1933.

## 1874

The year the club was founded.

## 76,588

Villa Park's record attendance for an FA Cup quarter-final against Derby County in 1946

Henri Lansbury

# ROARING ALL

## NOVA SCOTIA
## TORONTO

## CANADA

## REPUBLIC OF IRELAND

LEINSTER
MUNSTER
TIPPERARY
WATERFORD &
TRAMORE

## USA

| | |
|---|---|
| ARIZONA | LOS ANGELES |
| AUSTIN | MEMPHIS |
| BOSTON | NEW YORK |
| CALIFORNIA | NORTHWEST ARKANSAS |
| CHICAGO | NORTH CAROLINA |
| CLEVELAND | QUEEN CITY |
| DALLAS | SAN DIEGO |
| DETROIT | SEATTLE |
| FLORIDA | SPACE CITY |
| ILLINOIS | ST. LOUIS |

## UNITED KINGDOM

| | | |
|---|---|---|
| AMPERTAINE (NORTHERN IRELAND) | ISLE OF MAN | NUNEATON |
| AVIDS (DISABLED FANS) | ISLE OF WIGHT | PHEASEY |
| ATHERSTONE | KENT | OXFORDSHIRE |
| BARTLEY GREEN | KIDDERMINSTER | RUGBY |
| BERKS & BUCKS | KING'S NORTON | SCOTLAND |
| BLACK COUNTRY | KINGSWINFORD | SEDGLEY |
| BOURNEMOUTH | LONDON | SHREWSBURY |
| BROMSGROVE | KNOWLE & DORRIDGE | STRATFORD-UPON-AVON |
| DAVENTRY | LICHFIELD | SOUTHAMPTON |
| EAST ANGLIA | LONGBRIDGE | STUDLEY & REDDITCH |
| EAST MIDLANDS | MID-WALES | SURREY |
| EXETER | NORTH EAST | SUSSEX |
| GREAT BARR | NORTH WALES | WATFORD |
| GWENT | NORTH WEST | WORCESTER |
| HALESOWEN | NORTHANTS | YORKSHIRE |
| | NORWICH | |

# OVER THE WORLD!

*Thousands of fans attend every match at Villa Park – and thousands more follow the club's fortunes from locations all around the globe. The Lions Clubs – Villa's worldwide supporters clubs' network – now has around 200 branches.*

## EUROPE

ALGARVE (PORTUGAL)
BULGARIA
DENMARK
HOLLAND
FRANCE
GERMANY
LATIN (ITALY)

MALTA
NORWAY
SWEDEN
SPAIN
» ALICANTE
» COSTA BRAVA
» MALAGA

## UNITED ARAB EMIRATES

DUBAI

## BAHRAIN

## SINGAPORE

## CHINA

SHANGHAI
HONG KONG

## SOUTH AFRICA

JOHANNESBURG

## AUSTRALIA

ADELAIDE
MELBOURNE
NEW SOUTH WALES
QUEENSLAND

# all the answers...

## SPOT THE BALL (PAGE 53)

## WHO WEARS THE SHIRT? (PAGE 32)

| | | | |
|---|---|---|---|
| 1 TERRY | 4 KODJIA | 7 BJARNASON | 10 DAVIS |
| 2 TAYLOR | 5 HOGAN | 8 DE LAET | 11 AGBONLAHOR |
| 3 CHESTER | 6 HOURIHANE | 9 ADOMAH | 12 LANSBURY |

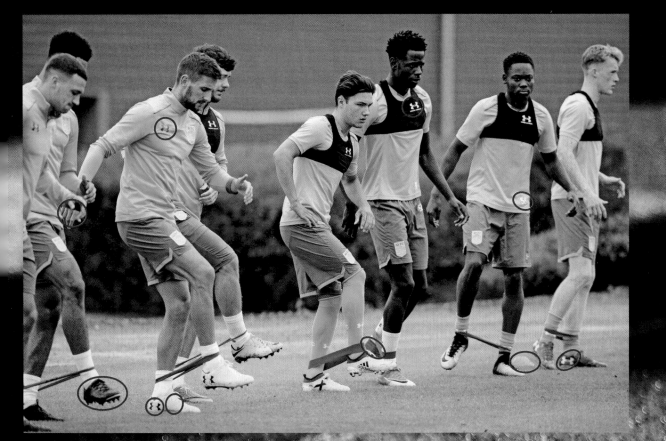

## NAME THE CAPTAINS (PAGE 31)

```
        J A S Z C Z U N
          B A R R Y
        S C H M E I C H E L
  M E L L B E R G
    T O W N S E N D
        R I O C H
        S O U T H G A T E
          P E T R O V
    L A U R S E N
  S T A U N T O N
          B E N T
  R I C H A R D S O N
```

### WHEN WAS THIS?
(PAGE 50)

1  (A) 1957
2  (B) 1961
3  (B) 1972
4  (C) 1992

### DO YOU KNOW CONOR HOURIHANE?
(PAGE 15)

1 (B) IRELAND
2 (A) BARNSLEY
3 (C) JAMES BREE
4 (A) BRENTFORD
5 (B) BRISTOL CITY